GOOD DAY, MISTER
GAUGUIN

CONTENTS

Painting on cover: Good Day, Mister Gauguin! (1889), detail.

Graphic design: Sandra Brys

First published in the United States
in 1995 by Chelsea House Publishers.

©1993 by Casterman, Tournai

First Printing

1 3 5 7 9 8 6 4 2

ISBN 0-7910-2811-9

ART FOR CHILDREN
GOOD DAY, MISTER
GAUGUIN

By Michel Pierre

Illustrations by Philippe Moins

Translated by Carol Volk

CHELSEA HOUSE PUBLISHERS
NEW YORK • PHILADELPHIA

 t all began in the mailbox of Mr. and Mrs. Redoux, apartment 4A. My name is Julian Redoux. Eleven years old and still wet behind the ears, as my older brother Sebastian likes to say. But my age doesn't prevent me from coming home alone every day from school. I have my own key to the apartment and my own key to the fateful mailbox.

That afternoon—it was a Tuesday during the month of May, I remember—I picked up the mail: two letters for my parents, a magazine, and a postcard. But the card was not the kind we usually get from the mountains or the seashore; this postcard had a picture of a magnificent painting on it, with three dark children sitting at a table spread with a large and a small bowl, a knife, and fruit. The children's faces were a little sad, and their eyes were staring, unfocused—like me, when I'm bored at school. On the bottom of the card was a name and a number: P. Gauguin 91.

Well, well, a mystery! There was no way that I could let a puzzle like this one pass me by! I have to admit that I love investigating, looking around, digging up what I can when I don't understand the name of a street, a monument, or a newspaper heading. So naturally this P. Gauguin interested me!

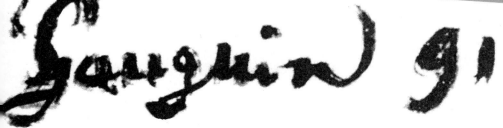

My first step was to check the encyclopedia. There I found 15 lines of small print, most of which I didn't understand. I did find out, however, that the painter, Paul (P. is for Paul) Gauguin, was born in Paris in 1848 and died in the South Sea Islands in 1903. I immediately realized that 91 must be the year he painted the children's meal—1891 that is—but the South Sea Islands were a mystery to me. I didn't know where they were, but I figured that Captain Victor, a friend of mine who lives in our building, must know.

Since I often show up at his door without warning, he wasn't surprised to see me, but he always has a slightly amused smile on his face around me, as if he didn't take me quite seriously.

"Captain, could you please tell me about the South Sea Islands?"

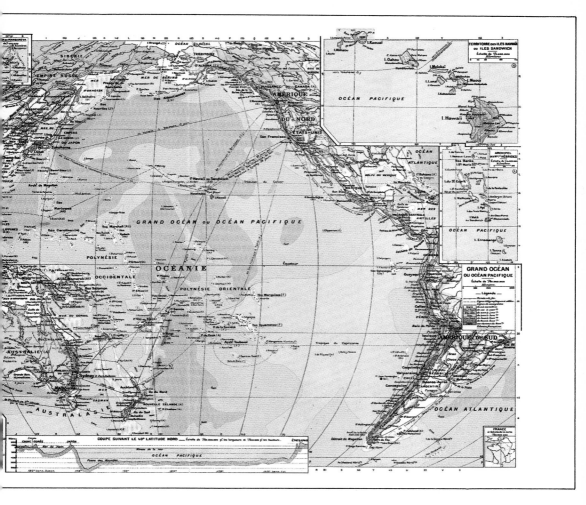

"That's a big subject! But come in and sit down at least. Why on earth are you interested in the South Sea Islands?"

"It's because of a painter who died there."

"Gauguin, you mean Gauguin?"

"Yes, did you know him?"

"Eh, my boy, I may be old, but I'm not *that* old! I was born 10 years after he died. But I sailed many of the same seas he did, for he was a great traveler.

"But let me start at the beginning. I'll tell you about Gauguin's life before he became a great painter. Look at these books!"

E ugène-Henri-Paul Gau-
guin was born in Paris
on June 7, 1848, at 52
Notre Dame de Lorette (now
no. 56) in the 9th arrondissement (Paris is divided into
twenty sections called arron-
dissements). His father, Clovis, was a journalist at the daily
newspaper *Le National*. His
mother, Aline, was a house-
wife and already the mother of
a little girl, Marie. The new-
born's ancestors included a famous maternal grandmother
named Flora Tristan. A fighter
for justice and freedom, a
writer, and a great traveler,
she was the illegitimate daughter of a rich Peruvian, Don
Marion Tristan Y Moscoso.
The family was also rumored
to be descended from Monte-
zuma, the last Aztec emperor.
It was no doubt in memory of
this ancestor that Gauguin,
many years later, nicknamed
himself the Indian.

**A ceremony celebrating the placement of a
commemorative plaque at Gauguin's birthplace.**

In 1849, when Paul was just over one year old, the Gauguin family decided to leave Paris and move to Peru. Clovis hoped to start a newspaper in the capital, Lima, with the help of the Tristan Y Moscoso family. But the journey proved fatal. Clovis died during a stopover at Port Famine, located at the mouth the strait of Magellan, in the south of Argentina. Aline Gauguin, now alone with Marie and Paul, reached the Peruvian coast fearful about the future. But she was warmly welcomed by the Moscosos, and settled into their large estate in Lima. The mother and her two children remained in Peru until 1855. Paul would remember his childhood in South America all his life.

View of Lima

Once back in France, the Gauguin family lived in Orléans at the home of their Uncle Isidore, Clovis' brother. Paul attended grammar school there, then classes at the small seminary.

In 1864, after a year of studies in Paris (where he mother had begun working as a dressmaker), he finished his schooling at the high school in Orléans. He dreamed of a profession that would enable him to travel. And on December 7, 1865, he embarked on the *Luzitano,* a ship destined for Rio de Janeiro, Brazil. While on board, he listened with fascination as a young lieutenant told him about the beautiful South Sea Islands.

Aline Chazal, Gauguin's mother

Paul Gauguin in 1873.

In October 1866, Paul Gauguin embarked as second lieutenant aboard the *Chili* for a thirteen-and-a-half-month-long voyage around the world. In July 1867, during a stopover in India, he learned of the death of his mother, who in her will entrusted her children to a friend, Gustave Arosa. The following year Gauguin began mandatory military service, spending the years 1868–1871 as a sailor aboard the *Jérôme-Napoléon,* which took him on a long tour of the Mediterranean, the North Sea, and the Baltic.

Gauguin's wife, Mette Sophia Gad.

Released from military service in April 1871 thanks to Gustave Arosa, a rich, well-connected man, he found a job at the Bertin financial agency, at 1 Laffitte Street in Paris. He becames what was called a "half-commission man"—which meant he acted as an intermediary between clients and stockbrokers. He excelled at his new profession, earned money, moved into an elegant building in the 9th arrondissement, and in November 1873, married Mette Sophia Gad, a young Danish girl living in Paris. Soon the couple had five children: Emil in 1874, Aline in 1877, Clovis in 1879, Jean René in 1881, and Paul-Rollan (nicknamed Pola) in 1883.

Peasant Girl with a Stick by Pissarro (1881)

At the home of Gustave Arosa, a discriminating collector, Gauguin started to learn about painting. He discovered the Impressionists and began drawing and learning to handle a palette and brushes. He showed real talent, earning him the friendship of the painter Camille Pissarro, who acted as his adviser. Gauguin devoted all his leisure time to this new passion. In 1876, he exhibited his work and began to form a fine collection of paintings by Paul Cézanne, Édouard Manet, and Pierre-Auguste Renoir. He participated in several Impressionist exhibitions, where he was noted favorably by the critics, and decided to dedicate his life to painting. He left the Stock Exchange and, in 1883, to his wife's dismay, abandoned his profession, declaring: "From now on, I shall paint every day."

Victor spent so much time talking and showing me books about Gauguin's life that I didn't notice how late it was. After promising Victor that I would return as soon as possible, I rushed home, hoping that my parents weren't worried about me. The following Saturday, I rang his bell. I was surprised to find him grouchy and out of sorts.

"No, my friend!" he growled. "This won't do. You say you're investigating Gauguin's life but I'm the source of all your information—I'm the only one answering your questions and showing you books!"

I was stunned. At first I believed that he really was angry, but then I realized he was just testing my skills as a detective. He took a folder from his desk and handed it to me.

"In here you have about 15 photographs of works by Gauguin with the date and place they were painted. For each of these I've written a short note for you. Now I want you to figure out when, where, and why he created these works. That's your first test. The second is to report back here with two maps, one showing the main places where Gauguin lived in Paris, the other the places he lived all over the world. You can also make one of the places in France where he traveled. I promise you a nice surprise if you succeed, but I doubt you will!" Victor added, laughing.

Well, of all things! I took it all in without saying a word and went home. My battle plan was simple! During the week, between my homework, friends, and school, I would plan my expeditions, and on Saturdays, I would execute them. He who laughs last, laughs best, Mr. Victor!

The first photograph, the first painting. A woman with children in a garden. On the back, Victor had written: 8 Carcel Street, 1882. The date was okay; I calculated that Gauguin was 34 years old then— that's the year he decided he wanted to paint every hour of every day and not just on Sundays. I checked a directory of the streets of Paris for the address: Capri, Capron, Capucines, Carcel. There it was!

The following Saturday, I headed out. I walked in circles until I found the narrow street with its dreary houses. But at the end was a pretty little square planted with trees on either side of a church. I felt a little uncomfortable but rang the bell of number 8 anyway. After a moment, a young woman opened the door.

From the Rue Carcel
(about 1882)

"Hello, Ma'am. I'm here because of Gauguin." In a few sentences, I explained the purpose of my visit.

She looked a little surprised but invited me to follow her down a hallway until we reached a magnificent garden that was totally invisible from the street! And this, I saw, was the garden in the Gauguin painting.

"Gauguin moved here in 1880," she explained to me, "at the invitation of one of his friends, who was also a painter. His studio was behind the glass windows, up there, and here he depicted his wife with their two little girls and their new-born baby, Pola, in his carriage."

I listened, jotting notes in a small book. When I left, I thanked her and stammered apologies for disturbing her, but I was pleased to have succeeded at my first test!

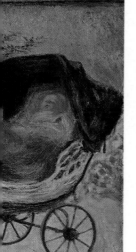

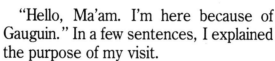

Gauguin lived on Carcel Street from 1880 to 1883. He painted his two daughters playing in the garden, Mette serving, and little Pola sleeping like a baby.

The second photograph depicted a fan with trees that are almost blue, boats on a river, and a bridge and a hill in the background. On the back Victor had written: the road to Rouen, 1884, 5 Malherne Cul-de-sac. Uh-oh! Paris is one thing, I live nearby and I know how to take the metro. But Rouen! On the map I saw that it was 75 miles west of Paris, on the banks of the Seine (at least that told me which river Gauguin painted). My parents would have never let me travel so far by myself.

So I had to tell them about my interest in Gauguin and Victor's challenge. But to fully convince them that the trip was worthwhile, I pretended that I had to give an oral report for school on Normandy.

My father eyed me suspiciously. He knew that I didn't usually volunteer for oral reports . . .

Still, the following Sunday we were in Rouen, the city in Normandy with the most monuments.

Influenced by the art of China and Japan, certain European artists — including Gauguin — took to painting fans.

I quickly found the Malherne Cul-de-sac (now called the Gauguin Cul-de-sac). I took a note that Victor had given me before I left from my pocket and read it at the very spot where the painter once lived: "Paul Gauguin moved to Rouen in late 1883. The cost of living was lower than in Paris, and he hoped to support his family on his savings until his first works sold. But after a few months, they ran out of money and Gauguin separated from his wife, who decided to return to her native Denmark with the children. The next winter, Gauguin returned to Paris along with his son Clovis, age 10. But they were so poor he could no longer afford paints, and he had to work as a poster hanger in the Paris train stations."

hen I looked at the third photograph I realized that my travels weren't over. It was a sketch of a little girl with a kerchief, a dress, an apron, and clogs. She is sitting in a field, her legs stretched before her, her left arm propped on the ground, her back turned slightly to the artist. The colors were mute, but there was a pretty red spot on her cuff. The date was 1886. The place was Pont-Aven. I had Mr. Victor now! I knew the place well. Every summer I spend a month there at my grandparents' house in Quiberon, on the southern coast of Brit-

tany. And I remembered having been to Pont-Aven and the surrounding area.

My investigation was all the more promising because I was going to meet my friend Mathilda there. She was a bit old for me, at least 25 years old, but I'd known her since I was little. She often watched me and took me to the beach.

Young Girl from Brittany, Seated (1886)

The walls in her house were covered with drawings, paintings, and engravings which her father collected. She had tried to get me interested in them the summer before, but I was more intent on swimming, fishing at high tide, or looking for shells at low tide. I resolved that this year, I was going to ask for her help. She knew a lot about painters and art history and had even been preparing for an examination to work in a museum. I had always thought her interest in art was strange, but now I changed my mind.

In Pont-Aven, artists, sailors, peasants, and millers mixed together. The streets were crowded and noisy with the sounds of the river mills, of carts heading for market, and of voices.

Finally, summer came. The first days in Quiberon I completely forget about Gauguin, what with the beach, my friends, and the sea. Then I remembered my search and I talked to Mathilde about it.

"Tomorrow we'll go to Pont-Aven," she immediately promised me, "but before we go, I'd like you to try to imagine what it was like for Gauguin to discover Brittany. A friend had told him that it was inexpensive to live here and that one could devote all one's time to painting. He had also spoken highly of the light, the beautiful sites, and the local hospitality."

"But why Pont-Aven rather than somewhere else?"

"Because it's particularly picturesque, as you'll see, with the river flowing into the sea, the mills, the old houses, and the nearby chapels. There were lots of painters there already."

"And were they all friendly to Gauguin?"

Gauguin took Madeleine, the sister of his friend Emile Bernard, as his model. He painted this portrait of the young girl, with whom he was in love, in 1888.

The light of Pont-Aven still plays off the reflections of the blue water, green shores, and white boats today.

"Yes and no. He didn't want to paint like the others. He was looking for his own style. He liked bright colors, sharp contours. He was critical and judgmental. Young painters (such as his friend Emile Bernard) listened to him and adopted him as their mentor. Gauguin advised them, but sometimes his bad temper got the better of him, and he made enemies too."

"Did he stay long?"

"Gauguin came to Brittany seven times, from 1886 to 1890, and one last time in 1894. He also took many trips and stayed for long periods in Paris, in France, and all over the world."

We went to Pont-Aven at about 10 in the morning and I must admit I was a little disappointed. It was so crowded with traffic that we had a hard time finding parking. But right away, I found pieces of what I was looking for: Paul Gauguin Place, Paul Gauguin Center, and posters of his paintings at the tourist office or on the cover of boxes of biscuits.

Above the book and school supply store I saw a plaque indicating that this was the inn of Marie-Jeanne Gloanec, where Gauguin and his painter friends lived.

Gauguin liked to walk the dirt paths of Brittany. Here he depicts himself being greeted by a peasant: *Good Day, Mister Gauguin!* (1889).

"It was a very cheap inn," Mathilde informed me. "Much less expensive than the hotels near the *Lion d'or* or the *Voyageurs*. There were a few rooms on the two upper floors and a restaurant on the ground floor, where the food was quite good. Gauguin wrote that the food could make you 'grow stout on the spot.' "

"But he didn't just eat and sleep, did he?"

"During good weather, the painters started their days happy as clams. They went off into the countryside, walked the path bordering the Aven, and planted their easels in the woods on the edge of the fields, near the mills."

"The peasants must have looked at them funny!"

"They had gotten used to them and were no longer surprised by these city artists. They all said good day when they crossed paths."

"Good Day, Mister Gauguin!"

"I think that's even the title of one of his paintings," added Mathilde, laughing!

In the afternoon, we took a long walk. Almost as if we were painters but without easels or paint boxes. All I had was a camera, which Mathilde helped me focus.

We had started the day by visiting the museum. It was a very bright building with old photographs and statements about Gauguin and all the painters who visited the region between 1860 and 1940. There are drawings, engravings, and paintings.

From the museum, we walked down toward the bridge and followed the Aven river. At one point, we reached an incredibly beautiful spot. On the left were large trees scaling up a hill and on the right the flowing river, the water crystal clear among the granite rocks.

"This is the Forest of Love," Mathilde told me. "It was the painters' favorite spot. The light plays on the leaves rustling in the wind, on the gushing water, on the changing sky. It's quite a challenge to capture such a site with paint."

The Vision After the Sermon, **also called** *Jacob Wrestling with the Angel,* **(1888) is the result of Gauguin's extensive experiments with simplifying forms and color.**

"How did Gauguin do it?"

"He painted this scene with broad stokes and bright colors, didn't worry about perspective, and defined the outlines of his drawing very precisely."

"Sometimes it looks like a stained-glass window," I said, trying to sound knowledgeable.

"Absolutely. Gauguin adopted a style called 'cloisonnism' or 'partionism.' It is like the stained glass windows in churches, where the colored glass is outlined by lead partitions."

Paul Gauguin in Breton dress in 1888.

**A**fter following along the river, we climbed a little path toward the top of the hill. I was getting tired! We walked for half an hour until we saw a small chapel. Mathilde was enjoying being my guide, and never stopped explaining the sites to me.

"This is the chapel of Trémalo. It was build more than four hundred years ago, and look how solid the foundation still is!"

We walked around the porch, admired the fine steeple and went inside the church through a small side door.

"Look at the wall facing us. If you look up, you'll see a wood sculpture depicting Christ on the cross. Gauguin knew this spot very well and painted that statue. And now, look at the picture Victor gave you."

The statue Christ that served as a model for Gauguin has been in the chapel of Trémalo for centuries.

"But Christ is yellow in the painting!"

"That's right! And here he's much paler but he's still basically yellow. That was Gauguin's style at the time. He took the color that seemed the most present and gave it full strength."

"People must have been surprised when he exhibited that painting."

"Absolutely! Not only that, but Gauguin sent the priest of the little village of Nizon (which is not far from here) a painting of a calvary that is found near the church. The good man was so shocked at the artist's style he immediately refused the gift, which he thought was the work of the devil!"

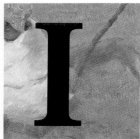**I** must admit that, in pursuing my investigation, I cheated a bit with Victor's documents. On Mathilde's advice, I put two photographs aside.

"Pont-Aven," she told me, "and a small port not far from there called Le Pouldu, are the places Gauguin frequented between 1888 and 1891. But he also returned often to Paris, and he spent some time in the West Indies and in the Provence region of France."

"He never stopped moving!"

"True, he always thought that somewhere else was better than where he was. And in April 1887, he set sail for Panama."

"Show me Panama on a map."

"It's right there, in Central America, at the narrowest point of the continent, between the north and south. But Gauguin didn't find any paradise there. He ended up as a digger on the work site of the canal that was being built to connect the Atlantic and the Pacific."

"He must not have been very well prepared for that work."

New colors, new light, new feelings: *The Mango Pickers*, painted in Martinique in 1887.

"Think again! Gauguin was a vigorous man. He was very muscular, with broad shoulders. But because of the living conditions and the climate he got very sick during an epidemic."

"Did he go back to France?"

"Not right away, first he spent a long stopover on the island of Martinique, in the Caribbean, to recover his health. Martinique amazed him. He was enchanted by everything and painted with great pleasure. Today we can get tropical fruits such as pineapples, bananas, and mangos easily. But think of how things were a century ago: most Europeans had never seen things from the tropics."

After Panama and Martinique, Mathilde told me about Gauguin's stay in Arles, in Provence, in the south of France.

"From October to December 1888, Gauguin lived in Arles, at the invitation of another great painter of his time, Vincent Van Gogh."

And as she was talking, she showed me one of Victor's documents. I suddenly realized that without Mathilde, I would never have progressed in my investigation.

"Look here," she continued. "Gauguin's most famous painting of the time is called *The Alyscamps in Arles,* named after a long path with antique graves alongside it. At the end of the path is a chapel with a strange steeple. You can also see the silhouettes of three women."

But when I looked at it I saw mostly greens, yellows, and reds swirling against a pale blue sky.

"Van Gogh admired Gauguin and was pleased to have him in Arles. But their personalities were very different, and at that time, Van Gogh was beginning to go a bit insane."

"They must not have had easy lives!"

"Things took a tragic turn. On Christmas night, 1888, Van Gogh approached Gauguin with a razor in his hand. He threatened him but did not strike him. Once back at home, however, Van Gogh cut off a piece of his own ear! The next

"I made a portrait of myself for Vincent. . . . I think it is one of my best works," Gauguin said after having painted *Self Portrait: "The Miserables"* (1888)

The sun, sky, and trees of Provence surround three women in *The Alyscamps in Arles* (1888)

day he was found with his head bleeding. He was bandaged and put away in an asylum for a few weeks."

"And Gauguin?"

"He simply went back to Paris, then on to Pont-Aven, and never saw Van Gogh again, who died two years later, without ever fully regaining his sanity."

By the end of July, I was pretty pleased with myself. On the pier of the port I had caught a fish that weighed over two pounds. At high tide I had collected two dozen oysters. I had also made progress in swimming, especially the breast stroke. In addition, my investigation was moving along. My maps of Paris, of France, and of the world were beginning to fill up with little dots and names.

One afternoon, when the Breton rain kept me inside, Mathilde found me looking over my maps.

"How's it going! Victor's never going to believe this, but now your investigation is going to be even more complicated."

"But I only have eight paintings left to track down—I'm half way through!"

"True, but those eight are the most difficult ones. They were painted in the South Pacific and I'd be surprised if your parents let you go there!"

"What should I do?"

"When your vacation is over, you should go to the Orsay Museum in Paris and look at the works Gauguin painted while on the South Sea Islands."

"But why did he go there?"

"He was looking for a different kind of place. He couldn't stand France any longer—no one seemed to recognize his genius. So in April 1891, after saying goodbye to his family in Denmark, he set sail for Tahiti."

"That's far!"

"Several weeks from Marseille by boat. He settled first in Papeete, the capital of the island, then in a little hamlet several miles away. The natives called him 'the man who makes men.' "

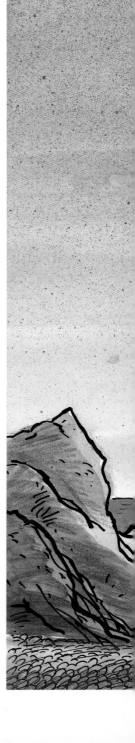

I had been to the Orsay Museum once already with my school class. I remembered that it was very big with works of art everywhere and a model of the neighborhood of the Opera underneath a glass sheet we could walk on. And we had also passed in front of lots and lots of paintings, but they had not interested me much. Perhaps the guide had even shown us some Gauguins . . .

So, the first Saturday after school started, I went back to the museum by

A red dog in the foreground, two women lost in dream, and in the background a venerated idol: *Pastimes* (1892).

myself, like a big boy. After asking for directions, I went inside and turned right, took the escalator, and arrived in the small exhibition rooms. In two of them were paintings by Gauguin. What a shock! Right there, before my eyes, were the three children with the table and fruit from the postcard that had started me on all this! I also found some works from the Pont-Aven period, and finally I found what I was looking for: a painting called *Pastimes,* which shows two women, one sitting with her legs crossed, the other playing a flute. I stood there listening to the other visitors, hoping to learn more. They passed quickly, bending down to read the name of the painting, then continuing on. No matter how hard I listened, I learned nothing new. I was about to leave when a gentlemen who looked like a tour guide arrived with a small group of visitors.

Gauguin abolishes the time and distance between Egypt and Tahiti.

Fresco from the outskirts of Thebes, around 1500 B.C.

approached discretely to hear better.

"When he arrived in Tahiti, Gauguin received a warm welcome from the authorities. But things quickly turned sour, and he found himself shunned. Few people understood his painting, and his regular visits to bars and other seedy places in Papeete attracted notice. He tried to learn their language, had a hut built, and settled in with a young local woman. He drew inspiration from the landscapes and scenes of daily life, although sometimes he borrowed images from other places and civilizations."

"What do you mean?" someone in the crowd interrupted.

"For example, Gauguin painted young Tahitian women sitting on a bench. But he chose to depict them in the manner of an ancient Egyptian painting."

I knew that! I had already compared this painting, which was among Victor's reproductions, with an illustration in my history book. I could even have added that the two men in the background holding the big fish were reminiscent of two Egyptian peasants carrying heavy sacks of wheat.

The Market (1892)

fter this success, things became more complicated. The photos showed some watercolors, but I could not find them in any of the cases at the Orsay Museum. I searched thoroughly, but to no use. I had to find another source of information. An idea came to me as I was walking in the vicinity of the museum. I followed the left bank of the Seine, heading toward Saint-Michel. I was looking for a bookstore that specialized in art books.

At the corner of Bonaparte Street I found a store that sells painting supplies, and right next to it I discovered a little bookstore, about as wide as a hallway. The facade was painted red so that you could not miss it, and it was called The Narrow Door—a perfect name! The window was filled with art books. I went inside—a less timid detective than before—and showed my photographs to the man behind the counter.

Watercolors from *Noa-Noa* (1893), a book of Polynesian beliefs and customs as told by Gauguin's brushwork.

"What you have here are reproductions from a book illustrated by Gauguin, which he put together during his return to Paris in 1893," he explained.

"He came back to Paris? After Tahiti?"

"Sure. He had done a lot of painting, but had sold almost nothing. After two years in the South Pacific, he was exhausted and penniless, and he headed back toward Marseille. He hoped to sell the 66 canvasses that he'd 'hatched,' as he put it. And he wanted to make a book with some drawings, photographs, and watercolors like the ones you're showing me. He wanted to call the book *Noa Noa,* which means 'the fragrant one' or 'the perfumed one.' That was the name he gave Tahiti, whose beliefs and customs he wanted to present while telling the story of his years there."

Design for the cover of *Noa Noa.*

41

he beginning of Gauguin's return to France seemed to take place under a lucky star," the clerk continued. "He was reunited with friends and people who admired him. And he was lucky enough to inherit a tidy sum from his Uncle Isidore, his father's brother. He rented a studio at 6 Vercingétorix Street, next to the Montparnasse train station. Here—if you look at this book, you can see a picture of the big house that he used as a studio and where he received his many visitors."

That was enough for me. The next Saturday, I went to Vercingétorix Street. I wandered around and around before finding my way. Today, on the very spot

Vercingétorix Street near Montparnasse at the end of the 19th century.

where Gauguin's house once stood, there are tall buildings and a modern hotel! I was a little disappointed—this was a far cry from the garden off Carcel Street I'd found at the beginning of my investigation! It was hard to imagine the painter in the middle of all this concrete. Luckily, that very day I received a letter from Mathilde with some new information.

Dear Julien,
I imagine that through your continued investigations you've learned of Gauguin's return to France after his first stay in Tahiti. But what you don't know is that he also went back to Brittany.
It was there, at this time, that he painted some of his most beautiful paintings.
Look in particular at the one called Breton Landscape: The Mill, dated 1894, which is at the Orsay Museum. You'll find in it everything I told you about in Pont-Aven: the colors, the harmony, the strength.
That said, don't let Gauguin interfere with your school work.
Mathilde

After sending the letter, Mathilde called me on the telephone one evening.

"I know I shouldn't help you so much, but I also have to tell you that Gauguin had problems during his final stay in Brittany. One day, in a brawl with some fishermen, he was knocked to the ground and kicked repeatedly with their clogs. Because of a foot injury, he had to stay in bed for several weeks, and he never fully recovered. To make matters worse, the young woman he lived with in Paris ransacked his studio. In addition, the sale he had organized of a large number of his works was a flop."

"All this happened at the same time?"

"Practically. In a few months, all the hopes he had placed in his return to France crumbled. So he decided to return the South Sea Islands and never come back."

"Until his death?"

"Yes, and in March 1895, after a final farewell banquet, he boarded a boat for Tahiti. This time he left without the hope of ever returning. He wanted to go back to the life, the colors, and the people he'd liked so much during his first stay. And this rediscovered pleasure radiates from

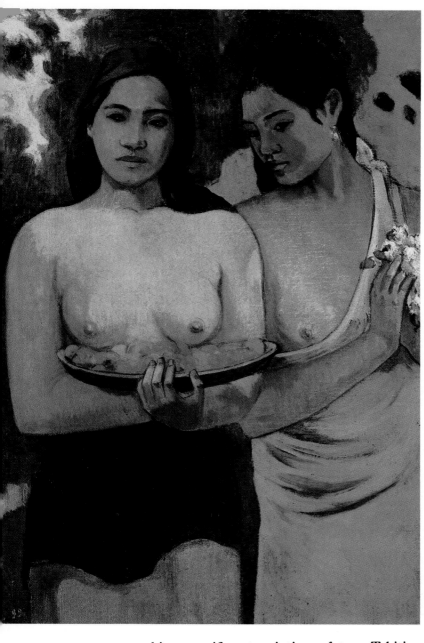

Tahitian Women with Flowers (1899)

his magnificent painting of two Tahitian women, with one of them holding a platter of red flowers."

"How did things go for him in Tahiti?"

"Pretty well to begin with, but soon his foot began to bother him again. He had to go to the hospital, and on January 3, 1897, he got some terrible news . . ."

Aline, his daughter

The letter Gauguin received from his wife on March 3, 1897, informed him of the death of his daughter Aline, on January 18, following a case of pleurisy. Aline was his favorite daughter, and her absence was most painful to the painter. Her face, with its fine features and melancholic gaze, had haunted his memory after the final farewell with his family in Copenhagen the previous year. At first he did not react to the news of Aline's death, but as the days passed his sorrow became unbearable. He wrote to a friend: "Ever since my childhood, I've been afflicted by misfortune. I've never had any luck, never any joy. Everything goes against me. It makes me want to cry, 'God, if you exist, I accuse you of injustice and incompetence.' "

Later he would also write: "Her name was Aline, like my mother's. . . . Her grave and its flowers only seem to be there. Her grave is really here, near me; my tears are living flowers."

The view from Gauguin's hut.

At this point Gauguin began thinking of committing suicide, but he wanted to complete a final work, his last testament as a painter, which he entitled *Where Do We Come From, What Are We, Where Are We Going?*

"Before dying, I wanted to paint a large canvas I had in my head, and for the entire month I worked feverishly day and night." He completed the painting on rough jute, a work almost 12 feet long and over 4 feet high! When it was finished, he left his hut, plunged into the nearby ferns, and poisoned himself with a bottle of arsenic. But the dose was too strong, and he vomited it all up. After a terrible night of suffering, he returned home. Death had rejected him. "Condemned to live," as he put it, he embarked on the final chapter of his creative work.

Where Do We Come From, What Are We, Where Are We Going? (1897)

Excerpt from a letter from Paul Gauguin to Daniel de Monfreid, February 1898.

"Before dying, I put all my energy here, an enormously painful passion . . . and such a clear faultless vision that whatever is hasty disappears and life roars. . . . On the bottom right, a sleeping baby and three crouching women. Two figures dressed in purple confide their thoughts to one another; one deliberately enormous, crouching figure raises an arm and looks in astonishment at these two characters who dare think of their destiny. A figure in the middle gathers fruit. Two cats next to a child. A white goat. The idol, its two arms raised . . . , seems to point to the beyond. The crouched figure seems to be listening to the idol; finally, an old woman near death seems to accept, to resign herself to what she thinks and complete the picture; at her feet a strange white bird holding a lizard in its claw represents the futility of useless words."

T he phone conversation with Mathilde was long but it was worth it. I also got to ask her for news about my friends from Quiberon.

I had reached the end of my investigation. It had lasted several months already—Victor wasn't going to believe his eyes when he saw my maps, my notes, and my keys to all the documents he gave me. Okay, so I had gotten a little help, but I did ask the right questions, look for books, and visit museums myself. I now knew so many things about Gauguin that I had left my big brother Sebastian speechless one night when he came into my room as I was looking at the reproduction of a painting entitled *Riders on the Beach*.

"So, worm," he sneered, "still looking at your smudges?"

I didn't like being called "worm" and I don't like Gauguin's paintings being called "smudges." I felt like calling him a creep but he was still too strong for me. So

Riders on the Beach
(1902), painted by
Gauguin near the end of
his life.

with my most knowing air, I decided to stoop to answering his question.

"This is one of Gauguin's last paintings. It dates from 1902. At that time, he was no longer living in Tahiti but on another island in the South Pacific, Hiva Oa, on the archipelago of the Marquesas, 750 miles from Tahiti."

Proud of this precision and seeing that my brother was impressed, I topped it all off with this:

"He arrived in Hiva Oa in September 1901 and had a solid hut build out of bamboos covered with coconut palms. Naturally he began painting again. But he was getting sicker and sicker. Of course, you wouldn't know about any of this, you numbskull."

I like to use that word to end discussions with my brother.

Under the Tahitian skies, *Breton Village Under Snow* (1894).

I had only one painting left, entitled *Breton Village Under Snow*. I didn't understand why Victor had put it at the end of his list. You would think the last reproduction would be a painting from the Marquesas Islands, not a work from Brittany! Not knowing how to deal with this problem, I decided to go back to Victor. After all, it was not unreasonable that he should help with the solution to this final puzzle. I deserved it, didn't I? I recopied my maps, assembled my documents, and found myself back in his living room.

"Mission accomplished, captain. You'll find everything in this folder. Except for this last painting. Why would he paint this snowy Breton village on a Pacific island?"

As I'd expected, Victor was truly surprised. I think he'd even forgotten his challenge.

"You amaze me, my boy," he said. "Congratulations. Now listen, Julian. I see you noted Gauguin's presence in Hiva Oa, in the Marquesas. He was enthusiastic about the splendor of these islands and painted beautifully there. But because of his eczema and heart troubles he was suffering more and more. The first days of May 1903 were the last of his life. On the 8th, he was found dead in his hut by his Marquesian friend Tioka, who began singing a funeral ballad in which he lamented the demise of 'the last of men.' "

I remained silent for a long while, imagining the solitary death of this man who had taken so much of my time for the last several months. It was all over . . .

"As for the *Breton Village*," Victor began again, "it's a painting that Gauguin never liked very much. He had painted it in 1894 during his last stay in Brittany and had brought it with him to the Marquesas. After his death, Gauguin's few furnishings were dispersed and his painting supplies and canvases, including this one, were sold at auction in Papeete. The auctioneer presented it upside down, no doubt as a joke, and called it *Niagara Falls*. As you can see, death did not put an end to the mockery Gauguin had been subjected to all his life."

When I went back home, all the images of Gauguin mixed together in my head. His life as a sailor, in Peru, Paris, Tahiti, Pont-Aven, the Marquesas . . .

Oh! I almost forgot the postcard with the three children. Now that I think of it, it wasn't addressed to me. The mailman had made a mistake, but I have him to thank for a wonderful adventure around the world and for the model Victor gave me—a miniature version of his boat! Talk about a surprise! I was really happy. Goodbye, Mister Gauguin.

Le Sourire, **the smile. An engraving for a satiric journal, made by Gauguin in 1899.**

Gauguin's Paris

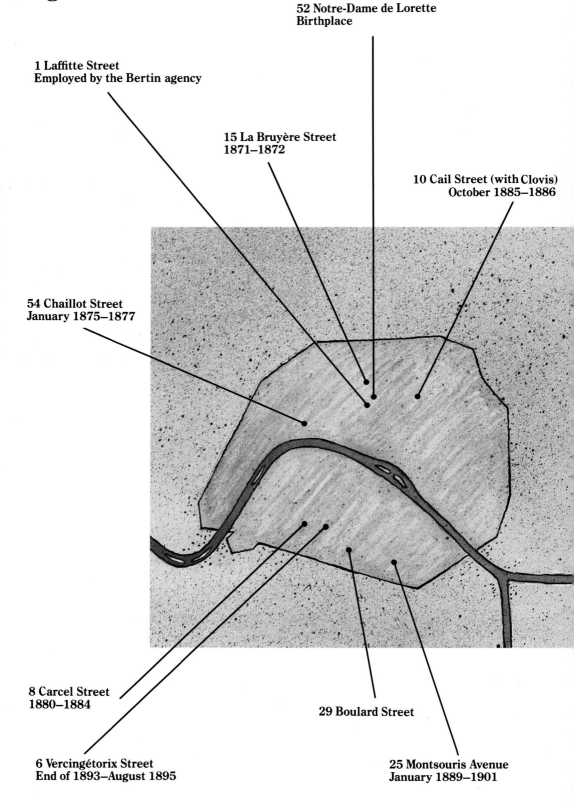

52 Notre-Dame de Lorette
Birthplace

1 Laffitte Street
Employed by the Bertin agency

15 La Bruyère Street
1871–1872

10 Cail Street (with Clovis)
October 1885–1886

54 Chaillot Street
January 1875–1877

8 Carcel Street
1880–1884

29 Boulard Street

6 Vercingétorix Street
End of 1893–August 1895

25 Montsouris Avenue
January 1889–1901

GLOSSARY

asylum: an institution for the relief or care of the insane or ill

Breton: of or relating to Brittany

Brittany: a province in northwestern France bordering the Atlantic ocean and the English Channel

calvary: an open-air representation of the crucifixion of Christ

Women of Tahiti (1891)

cloisonnism: a style of painting in which the shapes are outlined in dark colors, also called partionism

commemorative: created for the purpose of marking something by ceremony

eczema: an inflammatory condition of the skin marked by redness, itching, and lesions

epidemic: an outbreak of disease that spreads rapidly through a large population

facade: the front of a building

fresco: a painting made on freshly spread moist plaster

Gauguin standing in front of his paintings

Gauguin's drawing of two Polynesian gods, *Hima and Tefatou*

Impressionism: a school of painting that used dabs or strokes of unmixed color to simulate actual reflected light

jute: a rough, linen-like cloth

metro: the subway in Paris

Normandy: a province in northwestern France that is directly across the English Channel from England

perspective: the appearance to the eye of objects in respect to their relative distance and position.

Polynesian: of or relating to the islands of the south and central Pacific Ocean

Provence: a province in southern France bordering the Mediterranean Sea

satiric: marked by a biting wit that is used to expose foolishness

stockbroker: a person who buys and sells securities for clients

testament: an expression of belief or conviction

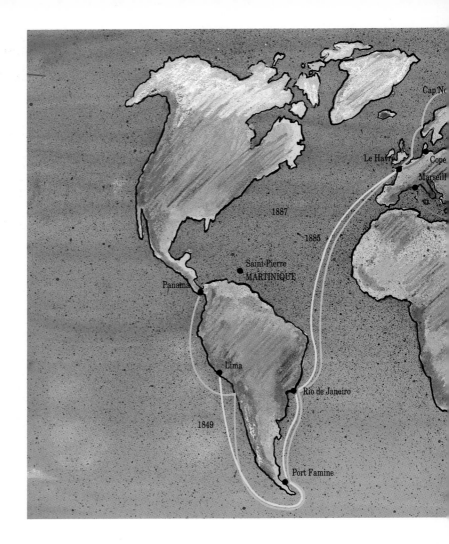

Chronology

———— : Gauguin's travels as a child

———— : Gauguin's travels as a sailor

———— : Gauguin's travels as a painter

1848: Eugène-Henri-Paul Gauguin is born June 6.

1851: The Gauguin family sets sail for Peru. Clovis, the father, dies during a stopover. Aline, the mother, remains four years in Lima with Paul and his sister Marie.

1855: The family returns to France. Aline settles in Orléans with her children.

1852–1865: Gauguin attends school.

1865–1871: Gauguin becomes a sailor, working first for the merchant marine and then for the military.

1871: Begins work as a "half-commission man" at the Bertin agency in Paris.

1873: Marries Mette Gad.

1874: Meets Camille Pissarro.

1880–1881: Gauguin develops a collection of Impressionist works and participates in the 5th and 6th exhibitions of the Impressionist group.

1883: Leaves the Stock Exchange in order to "paint every day." Quickly runs out of money and separates from wife.

1886: First visits Pont-Aven.

1887: Travels to Panama and Martinique.

1888: Stays in Arles with Van Gogh.

1891–1893: Lives in Tahiti.

1893–1895: Returns to France, staying in Pont-Aven and Le Pouldu.

1895–1901: Returns to Tahiti.

1901: Settles in the Marquesas Islands.

1903: Gauguin dies on the island of Hiva Oa.

Where are the works of Paul Gauguin?

Photographic Credits: